Sexy JESUS

Exchanging a Beautiful Savior for an Attractive "GOD"

Josh Mayo

A Youth Leader's Coach Publication

SEXY JESUS: Exchanging a Beautiful Savior for an Attractive "God"

ISBN 13: 978-0-9844158-0-9

3100 Briar Cliff Ave.
Fort Smith, Arkansas 72908
www.joshmayo.com

Cover design by Becky Siegrist of C1design.com
Back Cover Photo by Jody Rhoads of Memories by Jody

Published by Youth Leader's Coach
P.O. Box 450309
Atlanta, Georgia 31145
www.youthleaderscoach.com

Printed in the United States of America: Calvert McBride, Fort Smith, Arkansas.

For my father – Pastor Sam Mayo

Who looks more like Jesus than anyone I know.

UNSexy Thanks for *Sexy Jesus*

Soli Deo Gloria

Glory to God alone

My wife Monica Your beauty and grace is my daily reminder of what "Lordship" living really looks like. Your belief in me is as strong as your commitment to the Lord, and for that I am forever humbled. All my love!

Mom (Jeanne Mayo) I love you fiercely, and you are my inspiration. My words come from a lifetime of your influence and guidance. The following pages would not have been possible without you.
I.L.U.M.T.L.M.W.A.B.T.C.

Elijah (my son) Hearing you say "Dad" is God's sweetest gift to me. Any success I achieve in life or ministry will pale in comparison to the joy and pride I find in you. May I never make Jesus look "sexy" or cheap to you but model His eternal beauty and Lordship. I love you, E!

Justin You're the best brother ever. Thanks for showing me and the world the beauty of Christ in the sex-crazed world of Hollywood that you work in. You make Jesus real and authentic without compromising who He is. Thanks, bro!

Angie Kiesling I so appreciate your gift and time. You have crafted my words into a piece that I pray the Lord will choose to use for years. Thank you! By the way, can you edit these acknowledgments too?!

Elizabeth Vaught and Joey Barrios, Dan and Jenn Maciuk I so appreciate your selfless contribution to this book. Your time and suggestions helped this book become what it is now. You are a wonderful blessing!

The Alliance You serve and give your lives selflessly. I am honored to lead students alongside you. May we never take for granted the opportunity we have to make a dent for eternity. Following the Author and Finisher of our faith, let's change the world!

Craig and Sarah Johnson, Jon Morris, Greg Cultra, and Aaron Bettencourt You are the greatest friends and team I could ever do life and ministry with. Everyone knows you are the ones who make our ministry a success! Couldn't and wouldn't want to make this journey without you!

Pastor Marty and Becky Sloan Your belief and support in me is truly amazing. I am privileged to serve the Harvest Time family under you. Marty, you allow me to be me while pushing and enabling me to become everything God created me to be. I am honored to serve you.

Youth Leader's Coach Board: Mitch and Christine Soule, Lee and Janie Horner, Mike and Diane Rogers, Dan and Megan Valentine, Barbara Hardcastle, Ray and Debra Archer, Rufus and Berna Oladapo, and Judy Gregory Thank you for empowering the next generation of youth pastors and leaders. This upcoming generation will be different because of your selfless actions to be "Jesus with skin on." My entire family has been blessed by your support. You are some of our greatest friends! Thank you!

Harvest Time Elders: Roger Morris, Mike Moore, Ross Blythe, Patrick Tipton, Jimmie Deer, Mark Been I am so appreciative of your friendship and wisdom. Words cannot express my gratitude for your contribution and support into my life and the ministry I am privileged to lead. Thank you.

Alan Sowers I am beyond grateful for the countless hours and professionalism you have given to several of my books. Alan, you are a Godsend and I honestly don't know what I would have done without your support. You made this project your own and in doing so made me look sharp and put together in the process! I am humbled. Thank you!

Stephanie Robinson You have been one of the greatest blessings during this process. It has been a joy to work with you, and I am forever grateful for your contribution to the "physical makeup" of this book. Any author would be incredibly blessed to work with someone half as great as you and your team. Thank you!

Table of Contents

The tragedy of today's church world is that we've been called to **BELIEF** but not to **OBEDIENCE.**

1

Ever Feel Like Your Christianity Isn't Meeting Up to the 'Sales Pitch'?

It's the "dirty little secret" many of us don't have the guts to talk about. We give our lives to Christ and expect the whole universe to come alive with new meaning. Granted, the first chapter of our walk with the Lord is often filled with amazing changes and the thrill of personal relationship with Him. But somewhere along the way, we find ourselves secretly asking **"Is this all there is?"**

You know the internal questions because you've probably had some of them yourself. You were promised that Christianity would give you joy, peace, purpose, strength, and a whole list of other amazing gifts. And quite possibly you were promised some other benefits to your walk with Christ (everything from getting the dream marriage partner one day to getting other things on your "spiritual laundry list"). Nobody said much about *your responsibilities and personal end of the deal.* They just stressed all the *benefits* you'd get from your decision. In short, your decision to follow Christ was a pretty self-centered, no-brainer one. Who wouldn't want a free ticket out of an eternal roasting in hell? And on top of the fire insurance, you were told that Jesus would make all your troubles go away and give you the best life had to offer.

Yet somewhere along the journey, you secretly began to feel that your relationship with Christ wasn't really meeting up to the "sales pitch." Your troubles didn't all go away and those amazing "spiritual feelings" became less and less common. But the problem was even deeper than that. You found yourself feeling more distant from Christ than you wanted to admit. Your Christianity swung from degrees of boredom to times of internal restlessness and dissatisfaction. You maybe even toyed with ditching the whole thing; writing it off as just another aborted run at connecting with reality.

Then one day you stumble across the passage in the New Testament where Jesus tells His followers to "**first count the cost**" before deciding to follow Him. Hmmm...those words echo in your head. *You're not sure you ever did that. Nobody ever talked to you about the "cost" of truly following Christ.* They only gave you an amazing list of all the benefits (many of which are true). But on the day you chose to give Christ your life, He was presented to you as your Savior (Thank God!) and also as a spiritual version of the Tooth Fairy. I mean, He was forgiving you for your sins (Thank God again!) and then supposedly becoming your own personal "Bell Boy" to answer all your requests and get you out of jams. They sure didn't call Him by those names. But they definitely put the spotlight on all the amazing gifts that you were going to receive because of your decision. Quite a powerful "sales pitch."

Why do so many of us secretly say to ourselves, "Is this ALL there is?"

Now don't get me wrong. **There *ARE* more benefits to following Christ than I can ever begin to describe. He really does give us what John 10:10 calls "more abundant life."** But why do so many of us have unsatisfying relationships with Him? Why do so many of us secretly say to ourselves, "Is this *ALL* there is?"

It was my own internal questioning that led me to study the New Testament from a different perspective. In answer to Christ's directive to "first count the cost," I decided to study the Gospels to clearly understand Christ's "spiritual recruiting methods." And what I found really surprised me. Time after time, it was almost like Jesus tried to **talk people out of following Him!** He made radical statements like, "If you really want to follow Me, then pick up your cross!" He told other would-be followers, "The foxes have holes to sleep in and birds have nests. But the Son of God often doesn't even have a place to lay His own head." Then if that wasn't enough He said, "If any person decides to follow Me, he needs to first deny himself…because if a person wants to find true life, he first has to lose it."

"If any person decides to follow Me, he needs to first deny himself... because if a person wants to find true life, he first has to lose it."

Not exactly motivational, positive-advertising Jesus.

But the longer I studied the New Testament followers and Jesus Himself, the more I learned about authentic Christianity. Little by little, I began to see that the biblical focus of Jesus was **"Come to Me and GIVE."** That really threw me off. Because when I first became a Christ follower, people gave me the idea that it was more **"Come to Jesus and GET."**

So let's take this important journey together. My thoughts are nothing epic or original. Church leaders through the ages have spoken about them. But in our self-centered society where everyone wants their own speedy, cheap version of "McJesus" Christianity, I think this topic is central to our walks with Jesus.

Read with excitement and with intensity, because there really is a "more abundant life" in following Christ. He really does give us the mind-blowing, unmerited gift of forgiveness for all the garbage in our lives. But if your secret heart whispers, "There must be more..." then Jesus is about to give you a great gift.

What's my "bottom line?" **The epic message of the New Testament is surely "Jesus is *Savior*."** But you're going to experience an emptiness in your walk with Christ if you don't go further than that. **The life-altering emphasis of the Scriptures goes beyond "Jesus is Savior."** Read the New Testament through yourself and you'll see it with pretty staggering clarity. **The resounding focus of true Christianity is "Jesus is *LORD*."**

Did I just hear you say, "So what's the big deal?"

I understand the question. Just let me promise you that it's a big, big deal... especially from God's perspective. So let's take the journey together. It may open the door to the most wholehearted, exciting slice of Christianity you've ever experienced.

Because, you see, I don't think Christianity has been "oversold" to many of us. I just think that people forgot to honestly share the "count the cost" part. The tragedy of today's church world is that **we've been called to BELIEF but not to OBEDIENCE.** And that, my friend, makes ALL the difference.

Forget lots of other things in life. Just remember this:

Authentic Christianity really is FREE... but it's never CHEAP.

Authentic Christianity

really is FREE...

but it's never CHEAP.

2

A Computer Sales Guy Who Changed My Concept of Christianity

Trey was nineteen years old and just needed some cold, hard cash to make payments on the car of his dreams. Do you relate? He wanted to get into sales but his opportunities for the "perfect job" looked pretty slim. Searching through the classified ads, he set up his first real job interview. It was at a huge electronics store where Trey would join a sales force marketing high-end laptops and desktop computers. Lucky for him, though, Trey was also a "good talker." So within hours he sailed through the interview and was told to show up the next day for job training. That "dream car" was looking better by the hour.

Before going out on the floor for his first day of sales, Trey saw a sales video that pointed out the major computer models and their features. One high-tech laptop was highlighted on the video. It was the latest and greatest in modern technology. Even more important, Trey learned that this was the laptop that his performance and commission were most measured by.

"Sell enough of these new models," his manager said, "and your sales career here is golden! If not, you may be flipping hamburgers next week at McDonalds." So right after Trey concluded his two-hour training, he enthusiastically grabbed his sales "cheat sheet" and made his way to the computer section of the store. He was ready to make his millions.

Rehearsing his new sales pitch in his mind, Trey caught sight of his first prospective customer. He nervously introduced himself to the young woman and asked if he could help her.

"Sure," she said softly. "But I'm not exactly Bill Gates or anything. To be honest, I'm really stupid on this tech stuff, and I don't even know where to begin. I just need a new laptop for school."

The lights went on for Trey. He had his first victim. So he launched into his "no fail" sales pitch. The young lady grew more and more impressed as Trey demonstrated the computer's cool, trendy features. But it all came to a screeching halt when Trey eventually choked out the price.

"Man, that's way more than I can pay," the young college student said sadly. "That dollar sign is way above my budget. Sorry for wasting your time." And without another word, she turned quickly and left Trey's counter. Person after person that first day was wowed by Trey's computer sales pitch. But all their stories ended the same way. ***The price tag was just too high. They all left impressed with the computer but empty-handed due to the high price tag. Trey's first day on the job ended without one single sale.*** Late that night, Trey grabbed his coat and headed for home.

"Something's got to change tomorrow," he told himself. "I'm never going to get my car using THEIR sales tactics." So Trey stayed up late that night, re-engineering his own "new and improved sales pitch." Whatever it took, he was determined to become one of the store's top producers.

Sure enough, Trey returned the next morning with his own tailor-made sales approach. "After all," he thought, "I'm never going to get a car if I follow their lingo. I'll show these people what it takes to move computers."

Whatever his new approach, it worked like magic! People all over the store began to talk about the "new guy in aisle 5." By the end of his second day, Trey had sold SIX computers! On his third day, he registered EIGHT sales. And by the end of the week, Trey managed to break all sales records for the store. Twelve customers bought laptops from him before the store closed that evening! Everyone was talking about the "golden boy" in the computer department. Rumor had it that the regional sales manager was flying in the very next Monday to interview him on his new, unbelievable sales approach.

Monday morning when Trey arrived at the store, he was proudly escorted to the management office. People were beginning to treat him like the company celebrity. Just as promised, Trey was introduced to the regional sales manager, who flew in for a special meeting with him.

"Well, Trey, you've got the whole company talking, and so I had to come meet you myself," the manager said. "You have a bright future ahead of you here. But I've just got to ask you a question, young man. I hear you've developed your own special sales pitch for our new computer product. And whatever that sales approach is, we sure all know it's working! I've never seen sales like this before. Will you let us in on your secret?" So Trey proudly sat down with the manager and unveiled his record-breaking sales approach.

"Well, sir," he began. "The first day on the job was pretty discouraging. People were wowed with all the features and benefits of the laptop. I would log in and give them the demo, and they were ready to buy. **But every single sale fell apart at the same place: They all walked away when I told them the price tag.** ***In all honesty, sir, people wanted the benefits of the product but they were unwilling to pay the price."***

"So what changed after that first day, Trey?" the manager asked. "That's not unusual. The price tag is quite typically our biggest sales obstacle. How did you create this revolutionary turn of events?"

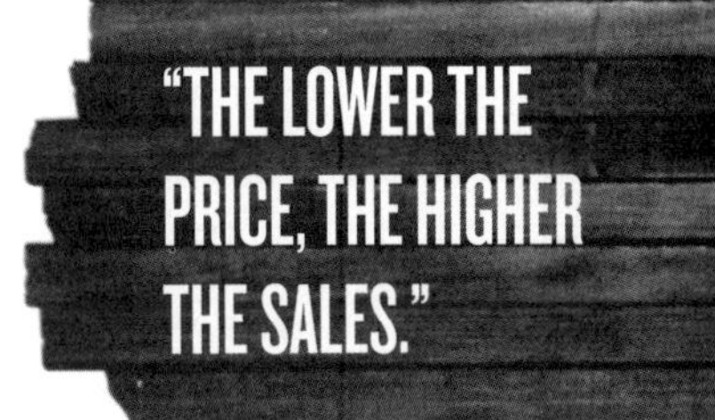

"Well, sir, the answer is really pretty simple. I decided that if PRICE was the problem, I needed to LOWER IT! So after the first day of such rotten results, I lowered the price of the model by 10 percent and my sales immediately started to go up. On the next day, I lowered the price tag 20 percent and the sales went even higher. I figured I was really onto something. So last Friday I sold the computers at 50 percent of the asking price, and the market went wild!"

The regional manager stared silently at Trey, stunned at what he had just heard. "You mean you kept lowering the price tag to get people to buy the computer?"

"Exactly," Trey proudly agreed. "Today's consumers are really interested in what we've got to offer. They just don't want to pay very much. SO THE LOWER THE PRICE, THE HIGHER THE SALES." Trey's answer was so simple. Too bad his sales career came to such a brutal halt. Even worse is that this philosophy has such big parallels in our walk with Christ today. Like the people at the computer store, we all want the BENEFITS of the product...but we're just unwilling to pay the price tag.

Agonizing. Even stupid. But isn't that a pretty accurate picture of today's world when it comes to Jesus? We're interested in His benefits and His blessings. We want all His happiness, His purpose, and His fulfillment—and we want them all "supersized." But when someone shares the New Testament price tag of "Jesus must be Lord," we back away from "the sale."

After all, we say to ourselves, we want a religion with glitz… glamour…and excitement. We want a pound of "Happy-Jesus," in a paper sack of convenience. Just don't ask us to pay a price that will cost us our self-centeredness, our materialism, or our pride. **WE WANT ALL THE BENEFITS OF A RELATIONSHIP WITH CHRIST—but at a highly reduced price. We want a SEXY, VOGUE JESUS…**packed in with all the contemporary, trendy extra features. We want a God who gets us new cars when we ask, amazing people to date at our request, and who takes away all our problems. But we want Him at bargain-basement prices. Cut out the "I surrender all" jazz. That's just not for us. Just give us the good stuff! Who would "buy into" Christianity if they realized that the "asking price" is "Jesus is LORD"?

So now, sadly, church after church follows the same pattern: "Come and buy our sexy, vogue Jesus! We're making Him available at rock-bottom prices. You can get all the benefits of a personal relationship with Christ without having to pay any of those unrealistic, demanding price tags of personal commitment, obedience, or sacrifice. We'll tailor-make Jesus to be the size and variety that best accommodates your own personal lifestyle and demands. We want to be able to announce in our next church newsletter how many 'takers' we had for our new, improved, sexy Jesus!"

And while we proudly tell others about our growing sales, Jesus leans over heaven to sadly watch the scene. He remains silent.

Probably because we're all too busy to ask His opinion on our new "sales approach."

We hear a sound—but then we block it out. We don't want to be inconvenienced by a guilty conscience anymore. The sound? We're not sure. But it sounds painfully like the Master as He watches us cheapen His death on the cross. Wherever the sound is coming from, it becomes undeniable. It's a deep, low groan. It's the groan of our brokenhearted Savior. His weeping gets so loud that we block our ears. There's nothing old-fashioned about us these days, not even guilt or repentance. After all, we're the POSTMODERN crowd. And look how our church scoreboard continues to climb.

There's nothing old-fashioned about us these days, not even guilt or repentance.

We numb ourselves to the Lord's pain. "Sorry, Jesus! We're just trying to make You more appealing to people so they buy into Christianity. Your old New Testament approach needs some help."

The sound of His crying becomes louder.

"Come on, Jesus. Get it together! This is the twenty-first century. We just want to help make You more attractive to this generation. They don't go for sacrifice anymore—they want glitz and glamour. Nothing sells without a little sex appeal. So let us handle this for You. We're Your new marketing agents. We're introducing You to this generation as the **"New, Improved, Sexy Jesus!"**

"Sexy" is slang. It means to make someone look highly appealing, interesting and attractive by means of a tempting outward appearance.

3

Are YOU Buying Into the 'Sexy Jesus' Trend Today?

For the past few years, I've been watching a trend that is picking up momentum FAST. It seems that today's Christian church is trying so hard to get "takers" that we are willing to do whatever is necessary to make the message of Christ relevant and attractive. Late one night, right before I crashed into bed, I was thinking about my own life. I have had my own share of personal compromises. As a youth pastor I have thought countless times that I've perhaps "mellowed back" the gospel. That night, as if out of nowhere, the phrase **"Sexy Jesus"** entered my mind.

I sighed. In that moment, I knew what the Lord was trying to say to me. My heart sank. I took out my laptop and began to journal some of my thoughts. Let me share a few of them that came to me that night:

*** "Sexy" is slang. It means to make someone look highly appealing, interesting and attractive by means of a tempting outward appearance.**

* Many of us, without realizing it, have tried to make Jesus look "sexy." Though we've probably not thought of it in these terms, we've tried to make Jesus more attractive and appealing to the non-believing world around us. Now that sure isn't bad. But the problem comes when we gradually forfeit standards, guidelines, and principles that the Word of God gives to us. Little by little, our attempts to make Jesus relevant can often result in creating a Christ that has very little in common with the Jesus of the New Testament.

*Authentic Christianity, when lived out to its fullest extent, is incredibly attractive and fulfilling. It's NOT just a bunch of rules and regulations. It really is "more abundant LIFE." But that "abundant life" also comes with other passages that say "Count the cost," "Pick up your cross and follow Me," and other pretty challenging scriptures. The trick is to get the "abundant life" without forfeiting biblical obedience to Scripture.

*It's like we're playing dress-up with God so that He looks more "cool" or easily accepted. We want to fashion Him so He easily gains the acceptance and approval of others. But in the end, He looks more like US and less like GOD. We've exchanged our beautiful Savior for an "attractive, appealing, sexy God."

We want to fashion Him so He easily gains the acceptance and approval of others. But in the end, He looks more like US and less like GOD.

4

The Wake-Up Call That Changed Everything in My Life

Please know that you didn't pick this book up by coincidence. I prayed that the right people would intersect with these pages. I'm not naïve enough to think I'll change how our society presents Christianity. But my heart will be at rest if I can even help impact a few of us (myself at the top of the list) to steer clear of the new, trendy "Sexy Jesus" approach that seems to be sweeping our society. Again, I'm not calling for anyone to become legalistic or condemning. I just want to encourage all of us to allow the New Testament to remain our guide along this journey. The Jesus we present to others must be the same amazing Jesus of the New Testament. He laughs with us...cries with us...and is altogether a Man like none other. But He is a Jesus with principles, standards, and character. When we minimize those aspects of Jesus in order to make Him more "relevant," we give a false picture of who He really is.

But here's the brutal truth I've come face-to-face with: *When I try to "dress Jesus up" to fit MY mold, I only give Him MY imperfections. If I really want Jesus to change ME, I have to stop trying to change HIM.*

Haunting words, aren't they? "If I really want Jesus to change ME, I have to stop trying to change HIM." Wow…only problem is that I'm not sure how I do that. So figuring out how to honestly let Christ take the steering wheel of your life is what this book is all about. I just want to explore with you how we sometimes (and often unknowingly) project Jesus through the vogue "sexy Jesus" lens and invariably cheapen Him in the process. It's sure not my desire to "dog" on Christians or the church. (There are more than enough books out these days that do that.) I just want to thoughtfully and prayerfully examine my own life in the light of God's Word. And it's my hope that you will decide to join me on that journey. The Bible is pretty blunt on this one. It says, "Judge YOURSELF or you will find yourself judged." So I want to do some thinking and some looking inside my own life, attitudes and motives before the Living God steps on the scene to do it. It's a never-ending process, that's for sure. I think that was what Paul was talking about in Philippians 3:13-14 (NLT).

When we minimize those aspects of Jesus in order to make Him more "relevant," we give a false picture of who He really is.

> I am still not all I should be, but I am focusing all my energies on this one thing: Forgetting the past and looking forward to what lies ahead, I strain to reach the end of the race and receive the prize for which God, through Christ Jesus, is calling us up to heaven.

What's the "prize" for me? I think it's getting a more accurate picture of the true New Testament Christ who has become the epicenter of my whole life. I don't want to gradually exchange my

"Beautiful Savior" for a superficial, flashy, twenty-first century version of God. And if you are one of the few people who think that none of this applies to you, let me challenge you to read on. You may be surprised to find that even the most sincere Christians among us occasionally try to make Jesus look a little "GQ."

You may be surprised to find that even the most sincere Christians among us occasionally try to make Jesus look a little "GQ."

How do I know?

Because, in an honest moment, I have to admit that I'm one of them. Thank God that truth, even when it hurts, really does "set us free."

When I try to "dress Jesus up" to fit MY mold, I only give Him MY imperfections. If I really want Jesus to change ME, I have to stop trying to change HIM.

5

Sexy Savior but Forgotten Lord

(The Chapter You Can't Afford to Miss)

A childrens' Sunday school teacher was trying to help the five-year-olds in the class know how important Christ's death on the cross for their sins was. She wanted to make sure that everyone understood HOW they could receive true forgiveness of sins. So after teaching the important lesson, she stopped for a closing review of the main principles.

"Okay, boys and girls," she said. "Can anyone tell me WHAT you have to do BEFORE you can get forgiveness of sin?'

The room was quiet for a minute. Everybody knew this was the "big question." Finally, a little kid from the back of the room thought he'd take a chance with his answer. He raised his hand sheepishly.

"Okay, Kurt," the teacher said. "What do we have to do BEFORE we can get forgiveness for our sin?"

"Well," Kurt slowly answered, "the way I've got it figured, the thing we've all got to do first to get the whole ball rolling is to SIN!"[1]

Let's be honest. If Kurt's answer was right, we'd all be in pretty good shape. I don't think I have any problem giving Jesus some "material to work with." If we define sin as where we "miss the mark" in following Christ through our actions, attitudes, motives, and behaviors, most of us have a pretty unending list. Thank God Jesus isn't looking for perfection or we'd all be toast! But biblical Christianity is more about our attitude than being "Polly Puritan" all the time. **It's fair to say that authentic Christianity is more about "DIRECTION than PERFECTION."** Our perfection is already found in Jesus Christ. So what is the "direction"—the mindset—New Testament, authentic believers are supposed to have?

The tragedy of the church world today is that people have been called to BELIEF but not to OBEDIENCE.

Obedience is the separating factor of true Christianity. Merely "believing" in Jesus Christ does not make someone an authentic Christian. If that's all it took, Satan would be a big believer himself! James 2:19 reminds us that the devil himself "believes and trembles." So if just making a "mental assent" that Jesus is the Christ makes you a Christian, the devil qualifies! Why is that a big deal? I guess it's pretty huge because we often water down Christianity to a shallow, mental assent that "Jesus is God." And when our sharing of the gospel goes no further than that, people experience a disappointing brand of Christianity. It's got to be more than merely saying, "I believe Jesus is God."

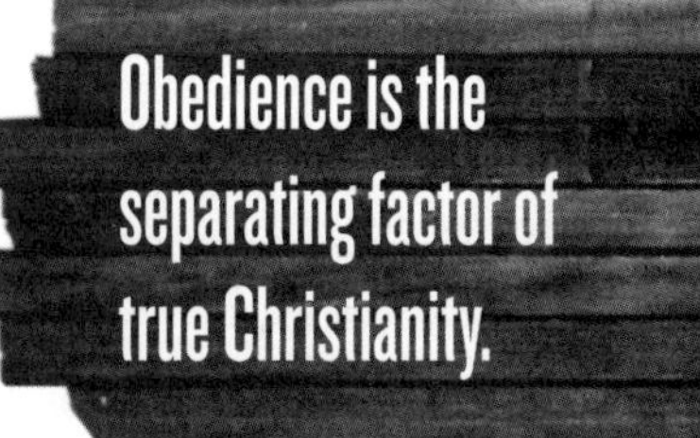

Acts 16:31 (NKJV) clarifies true, biblical belief. Its words should echo through our hearts as we walk the Christian life ourselves and try to lead others to authentic relationship with Jesus. It says, "Believe on the LORD Jesus Christ, and you will be saved."

Did you catch that all-important four-letter word? It doesn't read, "Believe on Jesus Christ and you will be saved." Instead, it reads, "Believe on the LORD Jesus Christ, and you will be saved." There's a huge, huge difference when you include that challenging little word "LORD" in the eternal equation.

I did a study on my own of the term "Lord" and came to realize that it's a pretty huge deal to Jesus. As I see it, the message of the New Testament is NOT "Jesus is Savior," but "Jesus is Lord." "Jesus is Savior" appears 24 times (ESV). But the far more repeated term is "Jesus is LORD." Drum roll, please. That appears approximately 500 times in the New Testament![2] I think the Lord is trying desperately to DEFINE who He wants to be in our lives in order for us to have a genuine relationship with Him. Jesus doesn't want to be just "mentally acknowledged." He doesn't want a "piece" of the pie of our life. He wants (and deserves) the WHOLE pie!

"Lordship": I think it is "AN END OF LIFE ON MY OWN TERMS."

Okay, so let me define the term "Lordship": I think it is "AN END OF LIFE ON MY OWN TERMS." So biblical, true Christianity is asking Jesus Christ into our lives for forgiveness of sins (that's the "Savior" part) as well as "LORD OF OUR LIFE" (that's the part people want to leave out of the equation these days).

Does that mean we have to be perfect to be a true Christian? Hardly! We'd all be toast if that were true. It just means that our mental outlook (our "direction") needs to always radiate from the reality that Jesus Christ is the LORD AND BOSS of our entire life. He is not only our Savior, but He is also our Best Friend, the One we most want to please, and the final Authority for all the decisions of our life.

How are you doing with that…really? Let's take a quick little quiz. The New Testament says that our "soul" is made up of THREE PARTS. So if we give our "soul" to Jesus, we obviously have to give Him all three parts of it. Your soul is made up of:

Your EMOTIONS + Your MIND + Your WILL = Your SOUL

So let's use that definition to see how we're doing on this exciting challenge of making Jesus truly LORD of our lives. Maybe it will help to make "LORDSHIP" more than a churchy word, but a reality we can constantly shoot for. Okay, now don't lie. Just ask yourself the following questions (and any other ones the Lord brings to mind):

***Is Jesus really the LORD of your EMOTIONS?**

I mean, do you refuse to let anger, insecurity, resentment, jealousy, pride, or other negative attitudes "take root" in your heart because you realize Jesus must be LORD over those feelings? Do you refuse to pout and feel sorry for yourself because you know that would not be His highest plan? Do you try to resist "bad mood days" because you know His plans for you are higher than passing, fickle moods?

Do you try to resist "bad mood days" because you know His plans for you are higher than passing, fickle moods?

***Is Jesus really the LORD of your MIND?**

Do you guard what you let into your head? Do you turn off TV and radio stations that start to send messages that are everything but Christlike? Do you use the great brain God has given you to accomplish some Christ-honoring goals? Do you walk away from conversations that become dirty, questionable, or gossip-filled? Do you turn off the internet when junk appears and it would be easy to secretly "keep looking" for a few more minutes? After all, nobody really knows where your MIND goes but the Lord Himself.

Now go easy on yourself here. We all have rotten stuff come into our minds. That's not the sin. The sin comes when we ENTERTAIN those thoughts rather than kick them out of our heads and bring them under the Lordship of Jesus Christ. I guess that's what the apostle Paul was talking about when he said, "I've learned to bring my very THOUGHTS INTO CAPTIVITY to the obedience of Jesus Christ."

***Is Jesus really the LORD of your WILL?"**

I mean, if your "soul" as talked about in the New Testament is made up of your "emotions, mind, and will," how are you doing when it comes to slapping your WILL into line? For me, some of the choices are pretty simple. I find myself consistently missing my "quiet time" with the Lord because I don't "FEEL LIKE" doing it. Or other times, I pass up opportunities to be kind to others just because I'm "NOT IN THE MOOD." I've heard all my life that "RIGHT CHOICES EVENTUALLY BRING RIGHT EMOTIONS." But that's sure harder to *live* than it is to *quote*. No, I don't think we have to "choose" to be a Christian all over again each day. But when the Scriptures say "Choose THIS DAY whom you will serve," we are being reminded that our MIND has to keep voting for LORDSHIP on a daily, ongoing basis. I know it's that way in my life anyway.

As I see it, the message of the New Testament is NOT "Jesus is Savior," but "Jesus is Lord."

6

Cardboard Cross Christianity

As a communicator, I'm constantly trying to make biblical principles come alive to my audience. Some of my illustrations are pretty cheesy when I look back on them. But let me share one of my illustrated talks that really hit the mark—at least in my own life.

Wanting to illustrate the principle of Lordship, I created a huge cardboard cross and awkwardly carried it onstage with me. I pretended to be a person who wanted all the BENEFITS of Christianity without any of the price tags. I wanted Jesus to get me a cool date, make me popular, solve all my problems, and just send me on my merry way. So I dropped by the "Salvation Counter" and picked up a "piece of salvation" at a bargain-basement price. (Some of the earlier versions had been too costly. But now I was ready to buy into some salvation because the price tag of daily obedience had been lowered. What a deal! I could have all the benefits of Christianity without the costly price tags of obedience to Him and surrender). I glibly picked up the cardboard cross and was merrily on my own way.

"What a sale," I said to the audience. "The abundant life of salvation without all those nasty, costly New Testament price tags."

But as my illustrated talk continued, I kept hearing the Lord's voice giving me "Lordship instructions." The Voice became pretty irritating. And, in truth, He kept pointing me back to specific commandments in His Word. Like once Jesus told me that I needed to apologize for my rotten attitude toward my family. But I didn't like that idea (after all, several people in my family had treated me wrong too). So instead of listening, I just took out a sharp knife and "cut that part of the cross off."

I just took out a sharp knife and "cut that part of the cross off."

"Give me a break, Jesus," I told the Voice. "I don't want a Christianity that demands that I apologize for my rotten attitudes—even to my family. We all get in bad moods. I want a Christianity that allows my moods and attitudes to be what I want them to be."

Then later on, as I was doing life with my cardboard cross, the imaginary Voice from heaven told me I needed to stop hanging out so much with one of my closest friends. That thought really ticked me off! Who did God think He was anyway? Telling me WHO and WHO NOT to spend my time with relationally? After all, I plan to get that friend saved someday. I know I've been slipping a little spiritually in front of him recently, but I'm sure not going to ditch him. Then the haunting Voice quoted Scripture again (it KEPT doing that!). It said quietly, "Don't be unequally yoked together in friendship with non-believers." Wow, what a rotten verse! How did that ever get in the Bible? So I held up my cardboard cross and began to cut off another big hunk of it. "Someone should have proofread the Scriptures," I thought to myself as I cut that part off the cross.
"I don't know how all those unreasonable demands ever got in the Scriptures!"

This process went on and on for quite a while. I kept cutting off the parts of the cross that I didn't agree with or didn't want to obey. "After all," I said to myself, "Sexy Jesus is the One that is appealing to people. Who is ever going to want a Christ that has so many guidelines you're supposed to follow? We all want the BENEFITS of a walk with God. But give me a break when it comes to biblical standards!"

Little by little, the CROSS was no longer in the shape of a true CROSS. I had cut so many pieces off of it that now all I had left staring at me was a large cardboard "I." And to make matters worse, the cross didn't "work" anymore! I mean, I tried claiming the promises of the Scriptures, but nothing happened. So in the illustrated talk, I looked for the Salvation Sales Counter so I could return my cross. I angrily told the "God-Mart sales attendant" that I wanted my money back—that my cross wasn't producing all the love, joy, and peace it promised in the ads.

I kept cutting off the parts of the cross that I didn't agree with or didn't want to obey.

But there at the return counter, with a cross that was now an ugly big letter "I," my mind remembered the acrostic for SELF:

Satan's
Exact
Location
Forever

Somehow I had gradually traded in the real cross for a big cardboard "I." Me, myself, and I...it was a lot different from the kind of Christianity I saw modeled in the New Testament. Jesus wasn't "LORD" in my current situation. In an honest moment, I had to admit that my true LORD was really the girl I wanted to date, the money I wanted to make, or the plans I was determined to carry out. I guess "LORDSHIP" wasn't "sexy" or vogue enough for me.

I even came up with a name for this disgusting form of Christianity. I now call it **"JOSH-ianity." Get it? Instead of "Christ-ianity," I've just slowly replaced Christ with my own name.** Painful but true. I think my new name more perfectly fits the brand of religion I often celebrate more than the old one. In an honest moment, I have to admit that I've put MYSELF at the center of most of my day-to-day choices, NOT Jesus. Anyone relate to me, or am I the only carnal Christian left out there?

If Christianity means Christlike, then "Josh-ianity" must mean a life that looks more like MYSELF and MY OWN SELFISH DESIRES.

I even went as far as to look up Webster's definition of "Christianity" in the dictionary. Here's what it reads:

> **Chris·ti·an·i·ty** (kris-chee-an-i-tee) n. 1. The Christian religion, founded on the life and teachings of Jesus.

Okay…maybe I'm getting a little extreme. But work with me. Following that definition, I often find myself pursuing:

> **Josh·ianity** (josh-i-an-i-tee) n. 1. The Josh (insert name) religion, founded on the life and teachings of Josh.

If Christianity means Christlike, then "Josh-ianity" must mean a life that looks more like MYSELF and MY OWN SELFISH DESIRES than it does Jesus Christ in all His Lordship. Man, that stinks! But I think it's pretty close to how many of us live our daily lives.

Okay, why don't you practice? I've been honest and it feels pretty freeing. Why don't you do the same thing, at least in your own private mind? Read the words below and fill in your own name:

> "More often than I would like to admit, I practice ______________________-ianity (insert your own name)… and make myself the High Priest of my own self-centered religion."

Right in the middle of my own reality-check, I read Exodus 20:3 in *The Message* version. It hit me pretty hard. God simply says there, "You can have no other gods, none. ONLY ME." I don't think He's saying that because He's insecure or jealous. Instead, He made us as human beings, and because of that God the Father knows HOW WE ARE GOING TO OPERATE BEST. So His Word is like a valuable "Instruction Manual" that comes with our life. He's saying to us, "I love you so much that I created you in the first place. Follow the guidelines in My Word and you'll experience the BEST POSSIBLE LIFE. Refuse and live life by your own standards and guidelines, and you are going to fall far short of the 'more abundant life' that I have created for you. But I gave you a free will. So it's all up to you."

No, God's not a "Cosmic Killjoy." He's not up in heaven trying to think of rules and guidelines to mess up our happiness. Instead, He is the Author of that happiness. His guidelines for life lead us TOWARD that fulfillment—not AWAY from it. But somehow we have a tough time really believing that. And it's especially tough when so few Christians around us REALLY choose to make the Word of God their daily standard for life. Just remember: God's not after PERFECTION. He's far more concerned with DIRECTION. He just wants us to make Jesus the true Lord of our life.

We'll mess up. We'll sin. We'll blow it plenty of times. He's not ticked with that, because His amazing grace covers us time and time again. He just wants to know that our heart and attitude is, **"Jesus, I totally belong to You. You are my Best Friend, my Lord, and my Master. Though I'm far from perfect, the bottom line for my life is that I'm learning, little by little, what it really means for You to be CENTER STAGE. Take me off the throne of my own life and put Yourself there, Lord. Only You are worthy of that position...and only You are SAFE in that chair."**

"Take me off the throne of my own life and put Yourself there, Lord. Only You are worthy of that position...and only You are SAFE in that chair."

7

A Famous Guy from History Talks to Me from His Grave

Sometimes it helps me to understand principles when I can find examples in history that make the principle clear. After all, "HISTORY" is really "His Story." So with that in mind, let me share a true story from the life of Alexander the Great. He was one of the most successful military commanders in all of history. By the time of his death, he had conquered most of the known world during the time of the Ancient Greeks. In short, he was one big, powerful guy!

One night Alexander couldn't fall asleep, so history tells us that he decided to take a walk along the edges of the camp that his men were guarding. To his surprise, he came across a young soldier who was sound asleep at his post.

Now what's the big deal with that, you might ask? Well, it was a HUGE deal if you were in Alexander's army. You see, the punishment for falling asleep on your post was immediate DEATH—no questions asked.

At any rate, Alexander the Great prodded the sleeping soldier and woke him up. The young guy looked up, petrified. He instantly knew that he was staring into the face of his commander-in-chief. Alexander was furious. Finally, he spoke to the young man.

"Soldier, what's your name?"

The guy stuttered, for reasons that soon became obvious. "My name, sir, is Alexander."

The commander was so angered by this answer that he took a minute to respond. Finally, in his harshest voice, he yelled into the darkness, ***"Well, soldier, either CHANGE YOUR CONDUCT or CHANGE YOUR NAME!"***[3]

The parallels are obvious. Our heavenly Father is looking down from heaven and saying to you and me, "Either change your CONDUCT or change your NAME. Either begin to get serious about obeying the directives of the New Testament…or stop calling yourself a Christian." It's not harshness that brings Him to that ultimatum with us. IT'S HIS MERCY AND LOVE. He doesn't want us to experience cheap "Cardboard Christianity."

It's not harshness that brings Him to that ultimatum with us. IT'S HIS MERCY AND LOVE.

Sexy as it may be to our self-centered world, He realizes that it is a "form of religion" without the true power of His Spirit. Christ wants us to experience the authentic…the genuine…and the eternal. And because of that He reminds us that true Christianity starts and stops with a heart that wants to gradually (one small obedience after another) make Him LORD of our everyday lives.

Someday when I stand before Jesus, I don't want Him to tell me what I "almost" did... what I "almost" accomplished for Him.

8

The Day Jesus Knocked at the Secret Closet in my Room

"Almost."

Isn't that a cruel word? Someday when I stand before Jesus, I don't want Him to tell me what I "almost" did…what I "almost" accomplished for Him. But there was a guy in the New Testament who lived in "Almost-ville." Let's read about him. I wish I could tell you that I don't relate to him. But if I'm truthful I relate to him far more than I want to admit:

> As he was starting out on a trip, a man came running up to Jesus, knelt down, and asked, "Good Teacher, what should I do to get eternal life?" "Why do you call me good?" Jesus asked. "Only God is truly good. But as for your question, you know the commandments: 'do not murder. Do not commit adultery. Do not steal. Do not testify falsely. Do not cheat. Honor your father and mother.'" "Teacher," the man replied, "I've obeyed all these commandments since I was a child." Jesus felt genuine love for this man as he looked at him.

> "**You lack only one thing,**" he told him. "Go and sell all you have and give the money to the poor, and you will have treasure in heaven.Then come, follow me." At this, the man's face fell, and he went sadly away because he had many possessions. Mark 10:17-22 (NLT)

Okay, I call this guy **The 13th Disciple** because he really could have been. And after reading that passage, I know a few things about this guy that make me feel like we have some things in common:

(1) He had done everything the law required for righteousness.

(2) He had never murdered, stolen, committed adultery, or even lied. Wow! He sounds like a pretty good guy to me!

(3) He even was a good son to his parents! It sounds like most churches would consider this guy to be one of their "leading saints."

But then Jesus looked at him and said those haunting words. I bet they echoed in the guy's head for a long, long time: **"YOU LACK ONLY ONE THING."**

Jesus went straight to the "closed closet door in his heart."

UGH. There it is. "ONE THING." Don't you think Jesus was being pretty demanding and picky? After all, the guy had done a bunch of right stuff and followed the Law. How come Jesus was zeroing in on one area of his life?

If we look through God's eyes, Christ's words here to the Rich Young Ruler were words of LOVE, not words of LEGALISM. You see, Jesus knew the guy's inner-heart enough to know that He was not really his true LORD. He knew that money was the real boss in his life. So, lovingly and wisely, Jesus went straight to the "closed closet door in his heart."

The Lord said firmly to him, "If you want this whole relationship between you and Me to work, you've got to go one important step further. I can tell that your money and earthly possessions are your true security. And I know that unless you allow Me to become your security, you will train-wreck your life. So go sell everything that you own and then come back to Me. It's only when you get rid of the possessions in life that hold you back that you will REALLY be able to follow Me wholeheartedly."

Unless you allow Me to become your security, you will train-wreck your life.

Now hear me out on this important point: JESUS WASN'T TRYING TO BE A TOUGH GUY HERE. His motives were all for the young man's good. **Our loving Lord understands that anything we allow to CONTROL us apart from Him will eventually DESTROY us. It is only Jesus Christ Himself who is safe to be in the "control seat" of our lives.**

I don't know about you, but I often have to stop and think about desires, people, or things that I have let become far too important in my life. I shove those areas into the "back closet," hoping Jesus won't notice. But then He eventually knocks on the door of my heart and reminds me, "Let Me have that—even what you have hidden in your heart's closet. It will eventually bring you pain and suffering if you don't surrender it to Me. If it's good for you, I'll give it back to you. But I'll give it back within the context of My Lordship over your life. That way, you will be able to ENJOY it—not be RUINED by it."

So what might be in the "secret closet" of your heart? We all have those areas. And I think they change from time to time. Let me give you some examples of things we stuff in the closet, attempting to hide them from the Lordship of Christ:

(1) **Our dreams for the future** (After all, we're afraid that God might have other plans for our life, and we are already sure what we want to do with it.)

(2) **Our attitudes** (After all, that person really did us wrong. We want to get even with them, and we're going to try to make that happen somehow.)

(3) **Our secret sins** (After all, no one sees where we go on the internet at nights when we're alone. God can't expect us to come clean with all that junk. Someday we'll get serious about mental purity—just when we get a little older.)

We never hear any more about this guy in the Bible. Does that frighten you? It should.

(4) **Our relationships** (Come on Jesus! Give me a break! I know this person isn't exactly Billy Graham, but I want to hang out with him. Someday I might even be able to ask him to church or something. I don't want to PUSH Christianity down his throat. Besides, all the Christians I know are geeks! If I don't hang out with this guy on the weekends, I'll just be stuck at home alone. No thanks!)

(5) **Tailor-make your own "secret closet."** The list is limitless. So just honestly pinpoint the areas in your personal life that you carefully compartmentalize. You know what I mean? We don't actually say it. But we live our lives about 95 percent surrendered to Christ and His Lordship. We just silently shut Him out of one "pet area" in our life. And little by little we start wondering why our "brand of Christianity" isn't working very well.

The end of the story for our would-be "13th Disciple" was a really sad one. The Scripture says that "He walked away—very, very sad." We have no indication that he ever decided to obey. He just kept making money and kept his possessions "center stage" in his life. He probably told himself that Jesus was being ridiculous—that someday he would give that stuff up. **Just not now.**

We never hear any more about this guy in the Bible. Does that frighten you? It should.

You see, the Bible goes silent on this "13th Disciple" because he kept the "closet door to his heart" closed in the area of finances and possessions. All the destiny God had planned for him—it never happened. All the dreams and fulfillment God had ordained for him—they never came to reality. Why didn't somebody tell this guy that "Jesus would be no man's debtor"? Translated: Why didn't somebody tell this guy that Jesus would always give us BACK far, far more than He ever asks of us? Why didn't someone help him realize that true surrender and obedience are the HAPPIEST, MOST FULFILLING WAYS TO LIVE? Why didn't someone remind the guy that Jesus just wanted HIM to own the possessions, not for the possessions to OWN HIM?

Jesus just wanted HIM to own the possessions, not for the possessions to OWN HIM.

Whatever the case, it didn't happen. The guy walks into New Testament history "very, very sad." And we don't hear any more of him. Wonder what he COULD have been? Wonder how amazing his life MIGHT HAVE TURNED OUT? Wonder what exciting destiny and dreams God wanted to live through him?

But none of it happened. *All because he wanted to hold onto his own "stuff."*

So let me ask you a tough question: *WHAT IS YOUR "STUFF"? I mean, what area is tough for you to totally surrender to the loving and complete control of Jesus Christ?*

Don't be embarrassed. We all have "STUFF AREAS." That's not the big deal. It's just about learning that we give those over to the Lord. He's such a good Dad. I promise you that. If your "stuff" will bring you ultimate happiness and fulfillment, He'll give your "stuff" back to you neatly packaged in His loving Lordship. Sometimes He gives back our "stuff," complete with strategic alterations to them. (You see, He sees into the future and knows the traps along the way like no one else can.) Other times He gently says, "Trust Me on this one. If I give it back to you, it will hurt you big-time along the journey. I made You, my child. Just trust that I care more for your happiness and fulfillment in life than anyone ever, ever could. So give this 'stuff' to me. One day you will be so very glad you did."

Our loving Lord understands that anything we allow to CONTROL us apart from Him will eventually DESTROY us.

9

End of All Your WRONGS or End of All Your RIGHTS?

I hear people say it all the time. "I don't want to give my life to Christ because I don't want to give up ________________" (fill in whatever self-centered sins or indulgences you want to add there).

But the longer I walk with Christ and study the New Testament, the more convinced I am of this very important fact:

"Relationship with Christ is NOT so much an END of all our WRONGS, but an END of all our RIGHTS."

You see, I used to view Christianity as this big long list of stuff I could and could not DO. But a quick read through the New Testament told me I had it all wrong. I remember the day I found Matthew 11:28-30 in *The Message Bible*. Let me share it with you:

> *Are you tired? Worn out? Burned out on religion? Come to Me. Get away with Me and you'll recover your life. I'll show you how to take a REAL REST. Walk with Me and work with Me watch how I do it. Learn the UNFORCED*

RHYTHMS OF GRACE. I won't lay anything heavy or ill fitting on you. Keep company with Me and you'll learn to live freely and lightly.

Wow! What a love note from the Lord! Yes, I'm often "burned out on religion." And He says that if I come to Him, I'll "recover life." I want to learn what He means by "UNFORCED RHYTHMS OF GRACE." When I'm trying to live under the Lordship of Christ, I can feel myself "forcing stuff"—trying too hard. Do you relate?

The more "rights" I turn loose of in my own life, the more true FREEDOM I find in my relationship with Jesus Christ.

He promises in this passage that He won't ask us to do anything that is "heavy" or that "feels like it doesn't fit us." BIG DEAL. So how do I get onto the train that teaches me how to "live freely and lightly"?

I think part of the answer comes in the words I shared earlier: "Relationship with Christ is NOT so much an END of all our WRONGS, but an END of all our RIGHTS." And before you begin to think that this whole concept just sounds "pretty heavy" again, let me tell you that it's really the doorway to freedom. Because the more "rights" I turn loose of in my own life, the more true FREEDOM I find in my relationship with Jesus Christ. It doesn't make sense, does it? But that's really how it works. The Bible says that if a man really, really wants to find TRUE LIFE, he has to first LAY DOWN HIS LIFE (mostly dealing with his own self-will and rights).

SO WHAT ARE SOME OF THE "RIGHTS" THAT SOMETIMES STAND IN THE WAY OF THE "UNFORCED RHYTHMS OF HIS GRACE"?

Well, I can only honestly share from my own life. Let me list a few and then you can make your own list:

(1) The right to be right…

(2) The right to my own time…

(3) The right to have people appreciate me for what I do…

(4) The right to be treated fairly…

(5) The right to be understood…

(6) The right to be accepted just as I am…

(7) The right for companionship instead of being lonely…

(8) The right to spend my own money any way I want to…

(9) ETC…ETC...

Get the picture? For me anyway it's really easy to say "Jesus is LORD" until that Lordship slips into one of the areas listed above. Then I quietly begin to remind the Lord that "It's not fair…I have a RIGHT TO ________________(you name it!)."

The only problem is that, one more time, I'm taking control of my own life. I'd like to tell you that your Christian walk will be free of moments where you'll feel like a "loser." But that's just not true. For a while, after you let go of your rights, you may feel like you are getting the raw end of the deal. BUT THAT'S JUST NEVER HOW GOD THE FATHER LETS THINGS WORK OUT!

Let me give you an example. My wife and I have a cool, amazing, young son named Elijah. He's only about one year old now. But let's fast-forward life a few years for him. Let's pretend he comes to me one day and says, "Dad, I really want to please you with my life. So I'm really going to try to be obedient to you in every area of my life. I don't want to run my own life because I know you and Mom are so much smarter and wiser. So take my life from this point on. I give up all my RIGHTS to you."

How do you think, as a parent, I'd respond to that kind of conversation from my son? Obviously, I'd first pick myself up off the floor from fainting! (Human nature just doesn't usually talk like that.)

Do you think I'd begin to take away all the things my son LOVES and will MAKE HIM HAPPY? Would I say, "Well, as your father, I take away your right to have fun outside…and your right to have cool friends…and your right to eat chocolate chip ice cream for the rest of your life"?

> Of course I wouldn't! **THAT KIND OF SURRENDERED, TRUSTING HEART WOULD ONLY MAKE MY PARENT'S HEART WANT TO TAKE EVEN BETTER CARE OF MY SON.**

And here is even better news: God the Father is a MUCH BETTER PARENT than I could ever be! So what am I trying to say? It's just the exciting awareness that the more you give yourself and your rights over to the Lord, THE MORE HE, IN HIS FATHER'S HEART, DETERMINES TO TAKE GREAT CARE OF YOU! That's a pretty amazing realization, don't you think? You really can't lose—just as long as you give not so much your "wrongs" but your "RIGHTS" to Him.

The more you focus on giving your "RIGHTS" to Him, the less powerful your "WRONGS" become.

And another exciting side-note: The more you focus on giving your "RIGHTS" to Him, the less powerful your "WRONGS" become. Don't ask me why. I can't really explain it. But when we focus on what we CAN DO, Jesus focuses on taking care of the stuff we "can't do." Isn't grace amazing?

"You are DEAD MEN. Now go out and prove it!"

10

Let an Old Communist Guy Help You Out

A guy named Douglas Hyde wrote a book that really marked my life. He called it Dedication and Leadership. It's out of print now, so let me tell you a little about it. Douglas Hyde was a high-ranking communist during the era when communism was taking over the world. He eventually gave his life to Jesus Christ. His book is especially interesting because he writes it from the vantage point of comparing Christianity to communism. At the time of his writing, communism ruled nearly 70 percent of the world.

Hyde compares how communism and Christianity present themselves to their potential followers. He quotes communist leaders like Kruschev, who said, *"So you want to join the Communist Party? Then all of you are DEAD MEN. Now go out and prove it!"*

Hyde's belief was that communist leaders had the guts to ask for TOTAL COMMITMENT whereas Christianity's leaders did not. In his book, he compares communism to the wholehearted call for commitment that Jesus Christ makes of His potential followers.

He says in his book: "While Christian leaders remained too apologetic to ask for radical commitment to the Christian cause like the New Testament relates, the Communists were not hesitant at all to ask for total follow-ship. The Communists said, 'Ask for LITTLE demands and you get LITTLE sacrifices. But ask for BIG demands and you will get BIG SACRIFICES.' So while Christians kept sugarcoating the call of the New Testament to 'pick up your cross and follow Me,' the Communists knew the power of that kind of challenge. The Communists routinely reminded people that life wasn't worth living unless you live it for a cause greater than your own. And in their eyes, that ultimate cause was Communism."[4] How tragic but profound that a converted communist would give this kind of exhortation to us as Christians.

Do you remember any of the stories from the history of communism? I heard often about people who were willing to walk away from their romances and their high-paying jobs so they could devote themselves to the communist cause. How agonizing to realize that God has hard-wired our human hearts to search for a challenge—to search for something worth being committed to. That's why He calls relationship with Himself "the Pearl of Great Price." It's the "something" in life that is worth the giving of everything. In another place in the New Testament, Jesus says, "What profit do you receive if you gain the whole world, and yet lose your own soul?" Those are some pretty heavy words. **TAKE A MINUTE AND DO SOME HONEST JOURNALING AGAIN.**

'Ask for LITTLE demands and you get LITTLE sacrifices. But ask for BIG demands and you will get BIG SACRIFICES.'

Obviously, we don't "earn" our Christianity by giving up things. Remember? He says in Matthew 11, "Come to Me…and you'll recover your life." But obviously the price tag of authentic LORDSHIP Christianity is a progressing level of obedience to the Lord's principles in the New Testament. That obedience will work itself into every area of our day-to-day life. So let me ask you another question: **What has it COST YOU to be a follower of Christ?**

Heavy question, isn't it? Do some serious thinking before you move on.

And while you're thinking, let me remind you of one of my favorite quotes, by martyred missionary Jim Elliot. It's the Mayo Family Mantra:

"He is no fool who gives what he CANNOT KEEP…to gain what he CANNOT LOSE."

So stop for a minute before you keep reading further. Let that quote echo through your mind and your heart.

Now take a little time to answer our thought-provoking question here: Up to this point in your life, ***"What has following Jesus Christ really COST YOU?"*** Just remember as you journal some of your honest thoughts: "**Christianity may be FREE…but never CHEAP.**"

"A religion that GIVES nothing, COSTS nothing, and SUFFERS nothing... is ultimately WORTH NOTHING."

Martin Luther

11

Jesus Calls You to Pick Up Your Electric Chair and Follow Him

Stories are great! Let me give you another one that relates to our topic in a "SEXY JESUS" society. There was once a chicken and a pig walking in a really poor part of town. As they made their way down Main Street, the chicken and pig continued to talk to each other. They were both sad because they saw so many people who were starving. There were even little children who seemed weak and ill because their parents didn't have the money to buy them food. Finally, the chicken came up with a bold idea to help the starvation problem in the little town.

"I got it!" the chicken said. "Tomorrow morning, let's both get up and serve them all breakfast. We'll give them bacon and eggs!"

The pig was thrown off by this request for a minute. But finally he spoke: "No way, buddy! ***For you, that breakfast would be SACRIFICE. But for me, it would be TOTAL COMMITMENT!"***

When Jesus recruited guys to follow Him while on earth, He didn't make it sound like an "egg breakfast." It was more like "bacon"—

everything or nothing. I remember as a young Christian reading Luke 9:23-26 (NASB). Christ's appeal was everything but "vogue and sexy." Listen to His words as He firmly called for "total commitment":

> And He was saying to them all, "If anyone wishes to come after Me, he must deny himself, and take up his cross daily and follow Me. "For whoever wishes to save his life will lose it, but whoever loses his life for My sake, he is the one who will save it. "For what is a man profited if he gains the whole world, and loses or forfeits himself? For whoever is ashamed of Me and My words, the Son of Man will be ashamed of him when He comes in His glory, and the glory of the Father and of the holy angels."

To "carry your cross" was like saying today **"Come and carry your electric chair!"** A person who was carrying his cross wasn't going to the grocery store or out for a date. If you were carrying your cross in New Testament times, you clearly were on one mission: YOU WERE GOING SOMEWHERE TO DIE.

No offense Jesus, but couldn't You choose a different analogy to get Your point across? This jazz about "carrying your cross" (your electric chair) sure doesn't come across real positive in our "have-it-your-own-way" world. I'm not trying to boss You around or anything, Lord. But someone needs to help You rethink Your public relations image and recruiting approach. Sorry, Jesus. But in the twenty-first-century, I don't think You'll have many "takers" with this kind of job recruitment!

But the Lord was much too wise to listen to me or my "sexy" counterparts in the Westernized churches of today. I remember years ago asking someone what it meant to "carry the cross" in my day-to-day life? The wise person thought for a minute and then said, "Josh, your 'cross' will usually be where YOUR WILL and the WILL OF GOD CROSS." Years later, that's still a pretty awesome answer.

When you choose to pick up your cross and follow Christ, you are essentially saying: "Lord, I know I'm not going to be perfect, but I want Your will to WIN in my life. PERIOD. Through the good and the bad, I want You to ultimately be in control of my life."

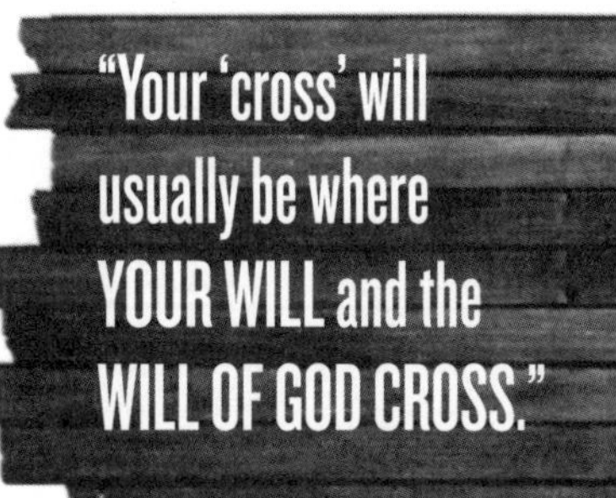

So what are some things that have been "the cross" for me? Wow, the list is pretty long. Sometimes it's my sarcasm and just wanting to make someone else look like an idiot with my sharp wit. Other times, it's choosing to forgive someone that I don't really want to forgive. (Come on, God! I can help even the score with a few people if You'll just turn me loose on that guy.)

Whatever the situation, you have the choice to either let Jesus be the true LORD of it or continue to "cut out pieces of your cardboard cross." While you're making your decision, just remember Martin Luther's powerful words:

"A religion that GIVES nothing, COSTS nothing, and SUFFERS nothing… is ultimately WORTH NOTHING."

Christ is searching throughout this world, not so much looking for DEAD SACRIFICES as for LIVING ONES.

12

Three Marks of a Dead Man

One of my heroes in the faith is a guy by the name of A.W. Tozer. He's one of those guys who challenges your thinking and level of commitment to Christ in positive ways. Recently I was reviewing some of his writings about what it means to be a genuine Christ-follower. Tozer talks unapologetically about the call of Christ in the New Testament to be "dead to self but alive to Christ." He shares three marks of a dead man. Let me share them with you. According to Tozer, you can recognize a truly dead man because he is:

1. **Facing in one direction**
2. **Not looking back**
3. **Making no future plans of his own**

Those three earmarks are pretty challenging, aren't they? How does your personal life measure up against these three traits?

(1) Would people who know you best say that you are ***"facing in one direction"?*** Or do you confuse those around you by your ups and downs spiritually? I mean, you start walking in a

Christ-honoring way but are constantly looking back over your shoulder, being double-minded on how focused you are on your kingdom pursuits. One day you are determined to honor Christ with your life and goals. But then, all too easily, your goals flip and your priorities become very different from "Thy kingdom come."

(2) Would your friends say that you are honestly ***"not looking back"?*** I mean, how much do you glamorize your pre-Jesus days when you are telling your personal testimony? And even more important, do you find yourself mentally "looking back" at your old life and wishing for aspects of it to return? Remember what happened to Lot's wife when she looked back at Sodom? God turned her into a block of salt! Why? Because when our EYES keep looking back, it's an indication that our HEART is still back there too.

(3) And third, would those close to you say that you are ***"making no future plans of your own"?*** There is surely nothing wrong with having goals, dreams, and future plans. But all of those future projections need to be regularly and sincerely given back to Jesus. The Old Testament prophet Jeremiah reminds us of Christ's promise: ***"I will give you a future and a hope"*** (see Jeremiah 29:11). But all along the way, *every* goal, dream, and plan are given back to the Lord Himself. That makes the future not only exciting, but also SAFE.

Let me go back again to talk about the legendary missionary Jim Elliot that I referenced earlier. On October 28, 1949, he wrote the profound words of commitment in his journal that I quoted to you: *"He is no fool who gives what he cannot keep to gain what he cannot lose."*

Jim lived out that short but powerful quote to the fullest extent of his life. He and four other missionaries (Ed McCully, Roger Youderian,

Pete Fleming, and their pilot, Nate Saint) made contact from their airplane with the cannibalistic Auca Indians using a loudspeaker. They used a basket from the plane to pass down gifts in order to build a relationship with the cannibals below. After several months, the men decided to build a base a short distance from the Indian village, along the Curaray River. There they were approached one time by a small group of Auca Indians and even gave an airplane ride to one curious native whom they called "George" (his real name was Naenkiwi). Encouraged by these friendly encounters, they made plans to visit the Aucas. Their dreams to share Jesus with this primitive tribe were ruined when a large, angry group of Aucas came to destroy them. On January 8, 1956, Elliot's mutilated body was found downstream.

As the years rolled on, both Jim Elliot's wife and children returned to do personal ministry to the very tribe who killed Jim. What an amazing legacy of commitment to Christ this man left. As Tozer challenged us, Jim Elliot lived a life *facing in one direction, without looking back, and with no future plans of his own.* Granted, most of us will never be allowed the privilege of giving our physical life for Christ. But Christ is searching throughout this world, not so much looking for DEAD SACRIFICES as for LIVING ONES. Are you up for the challenge?

Christ created me to "be played"—not to be a Christian diva whose every whim is carefully attended to.

13

What's Your True Focus: Supermodel or Servant?

Have you ever watched *America's Next Top Model* on TV? It really makes me laugh. If you're not familiar with the show, it's hosted by a supermodel named Tyra Banks. Tyra selects young women for her show and develops them into potential supermodels. At the end of the TV season, she awards one of these ladies with the "dream of a lifetime." It's a modeling contract that propels her into the turbo-charged New York modeling culture.

Week after week, Tyra runs a pretty grueling drill for the would-be models. She and her team give countless critiques on everything from how the girls should walk to how they should project their attitudes on the runway. Each episode, the contestants learn to look and act the part of a supermodel. From the brief segments I've watched, the girls are constantly changing everything about themselves just to be accepted by Tyra and the modeling industry. If the contestants are not willing to make the continual changes, they become "history" on the show pretty quickly.

Gradually, as the weeks of training pass, the "diva" begins to emerge in most of the contestants. Even off-camera, they demand immediate response to their requests and the adoration of those around them. Kind young women who entered the competition are progressively morphed into self-centered divas who seem to expect the universe to worship at the shrine of their personal desires and demands.

Let me ask you a question: Is it possible that as Christians we have begun to act like "spiritual supermodels"? No, I sure don't think Jesus wore Dolce & Gabbana sandals or carried His Scripture scrolls in a Louis Vuitton bag. But without realizing it, many Christians have begun to blend in with the self-serving attitudes of our supermodel culture. Though we all quickly quote Bible verses about servanthood, we are much slower to truly live out that mindset. The Words of the New Testament where Jesus says "the greatest among you are the servants of all" are no longer "cool enough" to be our daily mantra. Instead, we begin to slip into a mindset that focuses far more on our *PRIVILEGES as a Christian than on our RESPONSIBILITIES.* Whether we're male or female, Jesus must lean over heaven and shake His head sadly at our "Christian diva mentality."

We begin to slip into a mindset that focuses far more on our PRIVILEGES as a Christian than on our RESPONSIBILITIES.

And what kind of clear example did Christ Himself give us of this principle? It's my incredible honor to remind myself and you today that Jesus was a servant, not a self-centered "spiritual runway model." And that attitude of selflessness led Him to the cross where He gave His life for all of us. We've become almost calloused to the agonizing cost of His servanthood. Yet it challenges our priorities, our attitudes, and our responses every single day we claim to be a Christ-follower.

Matthew 20:26-28 in *The Message* translation puts it like this:

> "Whoever wants to be great must become a servant. Whoever wants to be first among you must be your slave. That is what the Son of Man has done: He came to serve, not be served - and then to give away his life in exchange for the many who are held hostage."

Excitingly enough, our choice to be a servant (to be "used" in the eyes of society) is often the calling card for the most fulfilling moments of our entire life. You see, in kingdom theology, when a person reflects the self-serving "diva mentality," they start to shrivel from the inside out. It's only as we consciously choose to live as unselfish servants to those around us that we are internally whole, fulfilled, and happy. ***Society calls it "being used." Christ calls it "being a servant."***

Many years ago, a renowned concert violinist named Niccolo Paganini died and willed his priceless violin to the city of Genoa, Italy. He left his legendary violin to the city with only one condition: The city leaders had to agree that no one would ever play the legendary instrument again. Paganini wanted to ensure the protection of the violin from anyone who might play it improperly. Even more, he demanded that the violin not be touched at all after it was mounted. He was determined to preserve its beauty and worth.

After an honoring ceremony, Paganini's violin was carefully mounted and put on display at one of Italy's epic museums. But a strange thing happened. Because the violin was pampered and never played, it slowly began to deteriorate. Year after year, its lack of movement allowed tiny worms to secretly begin their devastation inside the wood of the violin. But because of the city's commitment to never play or touch the violin, music lovers could only watch sadly as each year took a heavier toll on the once priceless instrument. Paganini's masterpiece eventually became a worm-eaten piece of decay. Why? All because it could not be used for its purpose—*it was created to be played, not carefully sheltered and unused.* If the violin could have continued to serve others through its beautiful music, experts say, it would have lasted indefinitely.[5] But unfortunately Paganini had a misguided "diva" mentality. And that mentality became the destruction of his dream.

Sometimes I myself forget that Christ created me to "be played"—not to be a Christian diva whose every whim is carefully attended to. He's called us to be servants and to lay our lives down in meaningful, practical ways for those around us. Sometimes that servanthood comes through a sacrifice of our time. Sometimes it is reflected in how we share our finances or how we lovingly reach out to others. Other own through private decisions to allow somebody else to gain the "upper hand" though we know they don't really deserve it. Whatever the avenue, Christians who focus on serving others become some of the happiest people to populate Planet Earth. Why? ***Because the person who is wrapped up in himself always makes a really small package.***

Most people wish to serve God - but they only want to help Him in an advisory capacity.

Most people wish to serve God - but they only want to help Him in an advisory capacity. What do I mean by that? Human nature secretly says, "I'll serve as long as someone gives me the title of leader or a head honcho." Even in Christian circles, we look for the spotlight or platform moments. We're secretly offended when we don't get public credit or applause for our supposed "servanthood."

In reality, **we piously call ourselves "servants" but get pretty ticked when people actually treat us like one.**

If the world could ever be won for Christ by our preaching, we'd have the job done by now! But I don't think the pulpit was God's main way to win the hearts and minds of others to Christ and His gospel. I think the Lord wisely knew how UNCOMMON attitudes of true servanthood are in society. So that's why He made servanthood the "gold seal" of real Christian leadership. Louder than Christian *words*, our acts of unselfish servanthood make the love of Christ real to everyone around us.

Christianity isn't so much about **PERFECTION** as it is **DIRECTION.**

14

Carried Any Manure Lately?

So how are you doing with walking out authentic servanthood in your life? If you're like me, you've got a long way to go. But, thankfully, Christianity isn't so much about PERFECTION as it is DIRECTION. (Remember?) Let me share a powerful true story from Christian history that echoes through my mind occasionally when I'm having a secret "diva moment."

One of Christian history's greatest leaders was a man named Watchman Nee. Though his impact for Christ was felt around the world, he based most of his ministry out of China. During the communist reign in China, he was tortured and imprisoned for his faith. After his release, he led a large group of Christ-followers to form a commune that was located on the outskirts of China.

Watchman Nee's fame was so significant that an American journalist flew to China to do a personal interview with him. When the journalist arrived at the commune Nee led, he saw hundreds of busy, hard-working people who were engaged in different tasks of farming. The members of the Christian group shared everything they owned with each other, from food to clothing to finances. The reporter was deeply impressed by the people. Not knowing where Watchman Nee's home was, he asked one of the men where he might find their esteemed leader. The man simply pointed toward a distinguished-looking older gentleman who was pushing a wheelbarrow full of manure, to be used as fertilizer in some of the gardens.

The American reporter was sure that the man had made a mistake. An influential person like Watchman Nee would not be moving manure from one place to another. After all, he was the spiritual leader of the entire nation of China at that time. Still desiring to interview Nee, the American reporter walked around the commune looking for its leader again. After walking around for another hour, he finally inquired of another Chinese farmer where he might find Watchman Nee. The Chinese man put down his shovel and personally walked the reporter to a location a few blocks away. "That's him," the farmer said. But once again, the person pointed out was the same gentleman pushing the wheelbarrow full of manure. Shaking his head in disbelief, the American journalist slowly walked toward the older gentleman and humbly introduced himself to the renowned leader.

Nee politely invited the journalist to his small apartment so they could talk with no interruption. After brief formalities, the journalist began to ask the questions he had outlined for the magazine interview. But about fifteen minutes into the talk, the interviewer could not stand it any longer.

"Pardon me, Reverend Nee," he blurted out. "I really need to ask you an important question. Because you are such a respected, world-class Christian leader, why are you personally pushing repeated wheelbarrows full of animal manure?"

Wise Watchman Nee sat back in his chair and thought a moment before answering. Then he said words that will forever define true Christian leadership for all of us who follow:

"Yes, that is true, son," Watchman Nee said. "*They* have made me their LEADER. And because of that, I have made *myself* their SERVANT."

Watchman Nee understood that true Christian leadership is much more like carrying manure than it is walking under spotlights on a runway. His example of selfless servanthood is a model that challenges all of us in the twenty-first-century Westernized church. It reminds us what real, authentic Christianity looks like on a daily basis.

So Tyra Banks, go ahead and make your millions. But my dream in life is not to walk a New York runway with the crowds snapping pictures of me. Instead, little by little, I dream of becoming less a "Christian diva" and more of a genuine, Christ-honoring servant. Perhaps one day I will learn to model the reality of Watchman Nee's powerful statement. It's a statement that strikes at the root of our "Sexy Jesus" generation:

"*They* have made me their LEADER. And because of that, I have made *myself* their SERVANT."

We make Jesus look sexy and cheap when we bail out during the tough times.

15

Three Guaranteed Steps to Make Jesus Look Sexy...

Step 1: How to Wimp Out Effectively When Things Get Tough

It was Christmas several years ago when I was finishing up my training for full-time ministry. But unlike all the holiday seasons before, this was anything but a "merry" Christmas in the Mayo home. Days before, my parents were forced to resign by a church deacon board at the church in Illinois where they had given thirteen years of wholehearted ministry. We learned that secret board meetings had been held without my dad and that they "wanted him out because the church wasn't growing fast enough." The whole thing felt like a really, really bad dream that we were going to wake up from and have it go away. My brother and I had grown up there. This was "home," and somehow it was being ripped unfairly away from us.

To make matters worse, my parents were determined to be godly through the whole mess. (Don't you hate it when that happens?) So they "resigned" to avoid a possible split in the church and told everyone on their last Sunday, "If you love us, you'll stay here and give the new leader all your support."

"Stay here and give support?" I thought to myself on the front row that farewell Sunday. I wanted all of them to bolt for the doors and close the church down! After all, my parents were more broken-hearted than I had ever seen them before. They cried themselves to sleep night after night. This wasn't at all what the reward of faithfulness was supposed to look like.

Fast-forward a couple of weeks. It was Christmas morning in the Mayo home, and I stumbled out of bed to follow the smell of cinnamon rolls my mom was making in the kitchen. We were alone, and out of nowhere I couldn't hold back the tears any longer.

"Okay," I blurted out. "I love you and Dad, but I've decided that this ministry deal isn't for me. I'm not tough like you guys. If this is how the church world rewards you for pouring out your guts year after year, then I don't want to sign up for the mission. I don't mean to hurt you, Mom. But I just can't do it."

Sound like simple words? Well, they weren't. I had told the world that I was entering the ministry since I was about four years old. While other kids dreamed of being doctors and lawyers, my plans never wavered. I just wanted to give my whole life for the cause of Christ. That desire and determination had never changed.

But now, that Christmas morning years ago, the bottom had fallen out of my world...and out of my heart. I was hurt beyond measure, broken into pieces on the inside, and deeply disillusioned with "the church." My brother even announced at Christmas dinner later that day that he secretly wanted to "pitch the whole thing with God" but couldn't because my parents were so "disgustingly consistent." In short, the Mayo family wasn't exactly humming "Have Yourself a Merry Little Christmas" that year. We felt a bit more like the "chestnuts" who were "roasting on an open fire."

Why am I telling you all this? Because those tough months were some of my most tempting ones to unconsciously make Jesus look "sexy."

I think it's really true that **we make Jesus look sexy and cheap when we bail out during the tough times.** By doing that, we nonverbally tell others that we can't depend upon God during the stormy seasons. He's not to be trusted. So although, Jesus might look good and sound powerful ("sexy,"), He's no one to depend on when the chips are really down.

During this unforgettable season in my life, the Lord made 1 Peter 5:8-10 (NASB) come alive for me. Let me share it with you:

> "Be of sober spirit, be on the alert. Your adversary, the devil, prowls around like a roaring lion, seeking someone to devour. But resist him, firm in your faith, knowing that the same experiences of suffering are being accomplished by your brethren who are in the world. After you have suffered for a little while, the God of all grace, who called you to His eternal glory in Christ, will Himself perfect, confirm, strengthen and establish you."

"After you have suffered for a little while?" Thanks, God…but no thanks! I'd rather pass up that part of Christianity. (Remember? With "Sexy Christianity" we get to pick and choose the portions of Scripture that we most like.) But with authentic Christianity, we come to understand the weight of these verses in 1 Peter. "After you have suffered for a little while, the God of all grace…will Himself perfect, confirm, strengthen and establish you."

That's a pretty tall order! He promises that when we don't bail out during the rough seasons, He will use those times to "perfect, confirm, strengthen and establish" us. That's a pretty staggering payoff for not taking the "sexy" low road during times when your world is crumbling at your feet.

It's not easy, I know.

It's just the TRUTH. Not a "sexy" one. But a very biblical one.

You see, our awesome heavenly Father sometimes allows us to go through deep, troubling waters in life not to drown us, but to mature and cleanse us. But if you're like me, I usually want God to do a "removing job" when I'm facing the rotten seasons in life. Here's the trouble: During the times when I want God to do a "removing job," He often wants to do an "improving job." Big, big difference. I've learned that to realize the worth of an anchor, you need to sometimes feel the fierceness of the storm.

To realize the worth of an anchor, you need to sometimes feel the fierceness of the storm.

Remember what James 1:12 (NASB) says. Let me remind you and myself:

> Blessed is a man who perseveres under trial; for once he has been approved, he will receive the crown of life which the Lord has promised to those who love Him.

Every time I read that verse, I think of the Olympics. In the earliest Olympic Games in Greece, the winners were given "crowns" rather than medals. I'm sure that's the word-picture Peter was trying to give us in this verse. But in the Olympics in early Greece, the marathon runners had a unique challenge.

You see, it wasn't enough for them to just cross the finish line first. In order to capture first place, each runner had to carry a lit torch for the entire marathon race. **So to receive the victory crown, the runner not only had to cross the finish line but cross it with his torch still lit!**

Wow! What a challenge to you and me. When the tough times come, we not only need to "keep running" but also fight to keep the fire of God's love and passion alive inside our hearts. That's no easy challenge. But the brutal truth is that **bad things DO occasionally happen to good people.** And unless we want to make Jesus look cheap and "sexy" during those times, we choose to put our game face on and learn what real endurance is all about.

> I learned not to confuse the fall of God's men with the fall of God.

As for me, you've already guessed the end of the Mayo Family Christmas story from several years ago. Little by little, I sorted through the junk, the unfairness, and the pain. I learned not to confuse the fall of God's men with the fall of God. And most of all, I steeled up the inside of my gut and determined **"I will finish the race."**

“Most of today’s Christian culture lives by the unspoken mantra “Sin now...Pray later.”

16

Three Guaranteed Steps to Make Jesus Look Sexy...

Step 2: How to Rationalize Sin and Make It No Big Deal

Okay, let's all admit it right up front.

WE ALL MESS UP. WE ALL SIN. OUR HUMAN NATURE STILL STINKS, AND FAR TOO OFTEN WE MAKE JESUS LOOK PRETTY BAD.

But what's the big deal? After all, most of today's Christian culture lives by the unspoken mantra ***"Sin now...Pray later."*** If Jesus is willing to keep forgiving our sins over and over, what's the problem?

Now if you are one of those super conscientious people like me, I want to remind you that Jesus IS unbelievably full of grace. As your Savior, He extends mercy and forgiveness to us a million times over—even when we repeat the same sins over and over and break His heart. Granted, we don't deserve that kind of forgiveness, especially when we keep wiping out in the same areas. But in reality **we didn't even DESERVE forgiveness the very FIRST time He gave it to us.** So it's just one of the most mind-blowing parts of relationship with Him.

But with that unbelievable mercy and forgiveness, it's really easy to slowly begin to "take advantage of God." Don't you hate it when people do that to you? I mean, we all want to give our friends a break from time to time. But none of us likes to feel taken advantage of or treated cheaply. That messes up the value of the whole friendship. I think that's what we do sometimes unconsciously in our relationship with Christ. Instead of remembering that we serve a HOLY God who wants to MAKE US HOLY, we shrink Jesus into our own self-serving image. We make Him "sexy" and trendy by blending His standards in with the standards of our society. After all, in our twenty-first-century Western culture, nothing is really "wrong or right." It's all "relative."

He's not trying to "fit in" with your friends. He wants to stand out.

Garbage! And while God vomits, we continue our mad pursuit to be accepted and popular with everyone around us. The only problem is that God isn't on that track at all. He's not trying to "fit in" with your friends. He wants to stand out. And if you are claiming to be one of His followers, He wants you to do the same.

How long has it been since you got really serious about some of your repeating sin patterns? I mean, it could be sins of attitude or sins of action. Maybe it's the insecurities you let eat you alive on the inside. Maybe it's your anger, resentment, or pride. Maybe it's where your mind goes or where you secretly visit on the internet. Or maybe it's your twisted set of priorities that makes romance or money too big of a deal.

You name your own repeating sin patterns. I know I still have plenty of it left in my own life. But I know something else. **There's a big difference between accepting God's grace and flippantly**

taking advantage of His love. One is biblical and worth the universe. The other is cheap and agonizing to the heart of God. Romans 6:1-4 in *The Message* reminds us:

> So what do we do? Keep on sinning so God can keep on forgiving? I should hope not! If we've left the country where sin is sovereign, how can we still live in our old house there? Or didn't you realize we packed up and left there for good? That is what happened in baptism. When we went under the water, we left the old country of sin behind; when we came up out of the water, we entered into the new country of grace—a new life in a new land!

People say that **"what we obtain too cheaply, we esteem too lightly."** Could it be that we don't take our personal sin patterns seriously enough anymore because Christ did all the "heavy lifting"? If so, when are you going to stop the excuses and the compromising? Your sloppy lifestyle is making Jesus look pretty cheap and sexy. His death for you on the cross was neither.

Your sloppy lifestyle is making Jesus look pretty cheap and sexy. His death for you on the cross was neither.

Let me share another story that reminds me that small, repeated sin can eventually cause big, big problems. A guy in a primitive town in Africa wanted to sell his house for $2,000. Another guy really, really wanted to buy it. But because he was very poor, he couldn't afford to pay the full price. After lots of bargaining, the owner agreed to sell the house for half the original price with just one big catch: *He would retain ownership of one small nail protruding from just over the front door of the house.*

Years passed and no problems came up. Then the original owner came back, demanding that the house be returned to him for an incredibly low price. The newer owner laughed to his face. He wasn't going to sell the house back to him *ever—and certainly not for that ridiculously low amount.*

The first owner didn't seem too upset. Instead, he had a plan in mind. He went out and found the carcass of a large dead dog. Unbelievably, he hung the dead dog from the single nail over the front door! The owner could do nothing about it. Legally, the first man still owned the small portion of the house that supported the nail. You've guessed the end of the story. Soon, the stench from the dead dog made living inside the house unbearable. People gagged every time they came anywhere near the place. One month later, the old owner had reclaimed the entire house as his own. Why? **Because he knew the power an enemy could have with just "one small nail."[6]**

If we give the enemy even one small "peg" in our hearts, he will eventually come back to hang his rotting garbage on it.

Repeated, willful sin, even when it seems small and "no big deal" ("one small nail"), eventually starts to STINK in our lives! If we give the enemy even one small "peg" in our hearts, he will eventually come back to hang his rotting garbage on it. And in the process, we give to the world a cheap picture of a "sin now, pray later" God. Pretty sexy, don't you think?

So are you progressively "dying to sin" or is it still a convenient option when you want it or feel like it will benefit you? Come on, friend. None of us are perfect. But repeated, willful sin in our life isn't a cute pet. In the eyes of God, it's the ugliest dog ever. ***So kill it…before it kills you.***

True love from a biblical perspective is the act of giving someone something they don't deserve.

17

Three Guaranteed Steps to Make Jesus Look Sexy...

Step 3: How to Abandon Authentic Love and Adopt the 'Feel-Good' Kind

What's your definition of "true love"? Most of us spontaneously think of romance and hormones. Love to us is when someone sweeps us off our feet and we ride off into the sunset. So maybe that's Hollywood's definition of love, but it's not the love I'm talking about. Christ's brand of love isn't a gushy feeling or a hormonal high. It's so super different from that. His world-class version of love is a fruit of the Spirit, not a self-centered "feel-good pill."

True love from a biblical perspective is the act of giving someone something they don't deserve. Christ's life shouts this kind of love—giving us all the grace, mercy, and forgiveness we sure didn't (and still don't) deserve. I don't know about you, but it would not be real tough for me to give love to people around me who "deserve it." But it's a whole different ballgame when I face off with somebody I secretly feel "doesn't deserve love." (I guess I think God died and left me in charge!)

My definition of love worked pretty well for me until I compared it to the Bible's. And then once more, I realized that I had adopted a pretty warped perspective. (Funny how that seems to happen so often in my life these days!) Listen to how Jesus spins this magical concept of "love":

> You're familiar with the old written law, "Love your friend," and its unwritten companion, "Hate your enemy." I'm challenging that. I'm telling you to love your enemies. Let them bring out the best in you, not the worst. When someone gives you a hard time, respond with the energies of prayer, for then you are working out of your true selves, your God-created selves. This is what God does. He gives his best - the sun to warm and the rain to nourish - to everyone, regardless: the good and bad, the nice and nasty. If all you do is love the lovable, do you expect a bonus? Anybody can do that. If you simply say hello to those who greet you, do you expect a medal? Any run-of-the-mill sinner does that. Matthew 5:43-47 (*The Message)*

Nothing like a little straight talk, Jesus! **"If all you do is love the lovable, do you expect a bonus? Anybody can do that. If you simply say hello to those who greet you, do you expect a medal? Any run-of-the-mill sinner does that. "**

"Grow up, you babies! You're citizens of My kingdom. Now live like it!"

Well, you can never accuse the Lord of beating around the bush! In a word, He was saying, "Grow up, you babies! You're citizens of My kingdom. Now live like it!" Live out your God-created identity. Live generously and graciously toward others, the way God lives toward you.

I'd like to propose a new definition of love for you to think about.

Authentic love is unselfish action toward an *undeserving* person.

When we just give love to people we like and people who DESERVE to be loved, we make God's love look sexy and cheap. We are nonverbally telling others that God only loves people who measure up—people who haven't crossed a certain invisible line. But that's not how Jesus set up this love business to operate in His kingdom. So let me ask you a pretty blunt but important question:

Biblical love is not so much a "set of emotions" as it is a "set of choices."

When was the last time you purposefully, consistently chose to give love to someone who didn't deserve it—someone who maybe really ticked you off or really hurt you?

And whatever your answer, that's a pretty decent measuring stick of how authentically you are walking in Christ's love each day. Are you smiling or sighing? As for me, I'm doing a little bit of both. Good thing biblical love is not so much a *"set of emotions"* as it is a *"set of choices."*

Let me close out this part of our discussion by sharing a true story from history that flies in the face of our "sexy" perception of love. It's obvious that the love Hollywood throws onto the movie screen isn't working in our society. Our divorce rates don't leave any debate on that topic. So let's take a look at how Jesus-style love can flesh out in our lives. Let me warn you though. It's not the self-centered, romantic, "feel-good" love that most of us want. Instead, it's a pretty costly one. But here's the good news. It's also a love that lasts and counts throughout all of eternity. Happy (and convicting) reading!

History talks about an unforgettable Baptist pastor named Peter Miller who lived in Pennsylvania during the American Revolution. (Miller was also a close, personal friend of a guy you've probably heard of: George Washington.) But living in the same city with the pastor was a negative, jealous man named Michael Wittman who spent much of his energy trying to oppose and humiliate the pastor. Year after year, Wittman made it his personal mission in life to destroy the influence and dreams of Miller in every distorted way possible.

As fate would have it, Wittman was one day arrested for treason and sentenced to die. When he learned of Wittman's fate, Peter Miller traveled seventy miles on foot to Philadelphia to plead for the life of this traitor. He found himself face-to-face with his friend, General George Washington.

Most of us give love and then require something in return.

"It's just not possible, Peter," General Washington said. "I cannot grant you the life of your friend, no matter how impassioned your request."

"My friend?" responded the old preacher. "He's everything but a friend. He's the bitterest enemy I have."

"What?" said Washington. "You've walked seventy miles to save the life of an enemy? That puts the matter in a different light. Yes, Peter, I'll grant your pardon." And he did.

Obviously, the pastor took Michael Wittman back home—no longer as an enemy, but as a friend.

So how are you doing in the "authentic love" category? Remember our new, biblical definition: **Authentic love is unselfish action toward an *undeserving* person.**

Does your brand of love run so shallow and self-centered that you make Christ look sexy and cheap to those who look on? In other words, is your version of love just being good to people who treat you right or who really deserve to be loved?

Think about it for a minute. Most of us give love and then require something in return. Society has a name for that kind of "for-purchase" love. It's called prostitution! Cheap…sexy…prostitution. In contrast, genuine love born out of our desire to follow Jesus as Lord is about a million miles in the opposite direction. It's a love that isn't for sale. We don't dish out love so we can get something in return or be treated in a certain way. Christ's words are pretty haunting on this one. He said, "Freely I have given to you, so freely give to others." Big challenge. Not very vogue, glamorous, or sexy. But it's the kind of raw, selfless love that sent Jesus to the cross for us.

So how are you doing, friend, on your self-evaluation? How "sexy" (cheap) are you making Jesus look in the way you live 24/7? Considering our "Three Guaranteed Steps to Make Jesus Look Sexy," I hope you're flunking. Unfortunately, most of the Christian world today is passing our three steps with flying colors:

Step 1: Wimp Out Effectively When Things Get Tough

Step 2: Rationalize Sin and Make It No Big Deal

Step 3: Abandon Authentic Love and Adopt the "Feel-Good" Kind

Just remember: You may make it to heaven with this cheap, sexy version of Christianity. But you sure won't take many people with you. Why? **Because you'll never CHANGE the world as long as you're LIKE IT.**

Holiness isn't just the ABSENSE of sin, but it's the PRESENCE of God in our lives.

18

A Closing Story You'll Never Forget

You're a rare person.

Know why I say that? Because only a person who wants to be above the "spiritual norm" would take the time to read a book like *Sexy Jesus.* Why? Because we not only want our Christianity to be "sexy," we also want our *reading* to be that way. And the challenging pages of this book have been anything but that. So thanks for being the kind of gutsy, authentic person who wants to do more than just fill a church pew and miss the weenie-roast in hell.

Just keep reminding yourself that this challenging business of "Lordship living" is a journey, not a destination. Almost every day of my life I miss the mark either in my attitudes, my priorities, or my actions. And like we reminded each other several times through the pages of *Sexy Jesus*, **God is interested in our DIRECTION, not our PERFECTION.** So don't let the enemy put you on the impossible spiritual treadmill of performance as you're walking out your relationship with Jesus Christ.

You see, if Satan can't neutralize you by having your Christianity one of only halfhearted obedience, then he'll flip the switch and try another tactic to get you out of the game. He'll take your sincerity and turn it into a constant, nagging guilt that you haven't been "good enough." He'll put the spotlight on all the areas you continue to mess up in. (And believe me friend, no matter how much you love the Lord, there will ALWAYS be plenty of those)!

Just remember that when it's the Holy Spirit doing the coaching, His voice will come with HOPE. He'll show you your shortcomings but He'll also give you the hope and strength to change. Holiness isn't just the ABSENCE of sin, but it's the PRESENCE of God in our lives. You'll feel MOTIVATED, not beat up. On the other hand, when the enemy is doing the talking in your head, he may sound pretty spiritual too. He may even point out stuff you're doing that REALLY DOES need to change (just not all at the same time). **But the enemy's voice will leave you feeling condemned and hopeless.** You've got to know the difference or you'll get so beat up and discouraged that you'll pitch the whole thing.

When it's the Holy Spirit doing the coaching, His voice will come with HOPE.

So let me wrap up our time together by sharing one closing story from history. It's about a monk named Telemachus who lived in Italy during the fourth century. He gives us a powerful picture of someone who refused the "sexy route" –someone who understood that if we're going to really change the world, we can't be like it. So let me leave you with his powerful story. It comes to my mind often when the "low road" is becoming too attractive in my own life.

Telemachus was a little, unknown monk whose responsibility in an Italian monastery was to tend the gardens. Over a period of months, he felt God continuing to prompt his heart to leave the monastery and go to the city of Rome. The quiet monk didn't know anyone in Rome. So at first he put the thoughts out of his head, thinking he was just making them up himself. But as the weeks went by and the impression grew stronger, he knew the Lord was really speaking with him. So, putting his few possessions in a satchel, he threw the bag over his shoulder and started out over the dusty, westward road to Rome.

When Telemachus arrived in Rome, people were running around the city with lots of excitement. He had arrived on one of the most celebrated gladiator fight days. The city was alive with the thrill of their barbaric entertainment.

Telemachus still didn't know why the Lord had sent him to Rome. He just understood that true spirituality is obedient, not sexy. So still without any answers, he began to follow the huge crowds of people who were packing into the Roman amphitheater that day. He had only a small amount of money, so his ticket was in one of the "cheap seats" near the top of the stadium.

When the gladiator fights began, Telemachus couldn't believe what he was watching. Time after time, two men would ride horses to the center of the ring. Then after the blowing of the trumpet, they would begin a sword fight to the death. The victor would live and be cheered. But the defeated man would die a public death in the sand of the arena, with his blood spilling to the ground, while the barbaric crowd shouted chants of merriment. He sat there, disbelieving, while the eighty thousand participants cheered "Hail, Caesar! We die to the glory of Caesar!" Finally, Telemachus could not stand to stay in his seat any longer. In his heart of hearts, he believed that God had sent him to Rome for this moment.

Telemachus got up from his top-balcony seat and began to make his way down the steps. He started yelling frantically at the top of his lungs, **"In the name of Christ, I beg you...STOP!"** The crowd seated near him in the huge stadium began to jeer and make fun of the simple-minded monk, but he continued just the same.

Making his way down to the bottom of his seating level, he looked around at his section of the massive amphitheater and continued to yell, "In the name of Christ, I beg you… STOP!" But there were thousands of yelling people at the gladiator fight, and only a few hundred could possibly hear his pleading words. He agonized as another man fell off his horse, a sword protruding from his chest and blood gushing from his body. The hideous cruelty of it all ripped at his heart. Yet the massive crowd cheered loudly again, being entertained at the death of another human being. **Sexy entertainment. (Much like a lot of ours today, wouldn't you say?)**

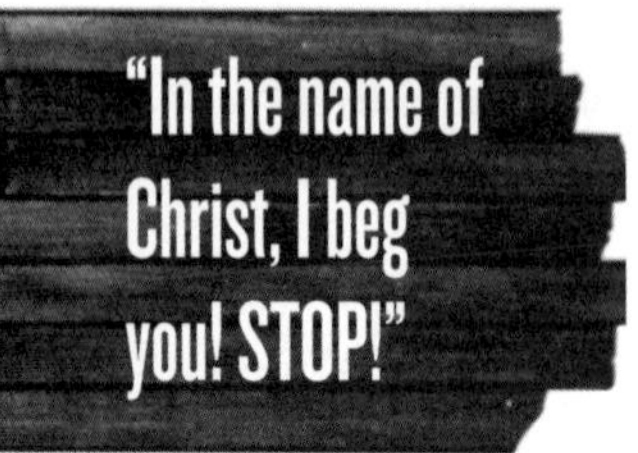

Finally Telemachus made his way to the edge of the wall that led into the arena fighting floor. Awkwardly, he crawled over the wall and into the center of the arena. By this time the crowd thought he was part of the act. They laughed and began to cheer for him, thinking he was a clown dressed up as a monk for part of the show. He ran around to all sides of the massive arena, screaming from the top of his lungs. Yet the more he begged them to stop, the louder they chanted for the next fight to begin.

Moments later, the next two Roman gladiators rode to the center of the field to begin their agonizing fate. Telemachus didn't know what to do. He only knew that what was happening was wrong and that someone had to attempt a change. So, courageously, he came to stand between the two gladiators right before they began their sword fight. Putting his hands up toward both of them, Telemachus said to the men, **"In the name of Christ, I beg you! STOP!"**

While the crowds chanted merrily, the tension in the center of the arena was excruciating. Both men knew they were perhaps not going to see the light of another day. So neither of them was in the mood to patiently endure a little monk and his pleading request.

They cursed at him, demanding that he leave the field. But Telemachus refused the "sexy, easy" response. No. What God had called him to *was not easy, but it was right.* So he steeled himself and stood his ground between the men. Once more, he looked up into their tense faces and shouted, **"In the name of Christ, I beg you! STOP!"**

One of the gladiators snapped. He could no longer tolerate this ridiculous little monk preaching sermons to him at the possible gate of his own grave. So without words, he angrily thrust his sword through the stomach of Telemachus, sending him to the ground.

The crowd began to silence. In that moment, they came to realize that the little monk was far more than a clown for the show. A hush came over the entire amphitheater as Telemachus tried pitifully to crawl from the arena. Blood gushed from his body. He collapsed just yards from the gladiators and took his final breath.

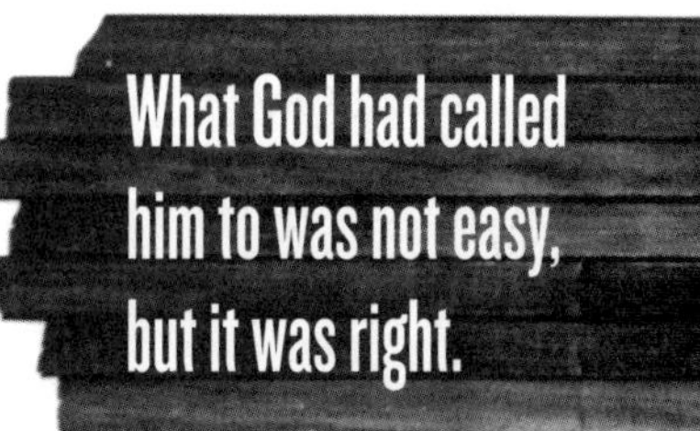

Slowly, the tiers of the amphitheater began to empty. **Tens of thousands of people who had just been shouting "Hail, Caesar!" now stood in silence. They had watched a humble monk "shout" even louder with the obedience of his life. The "volume" of this one man's obedience to Christ became almost deafening to their hardened, "sexy" human hearts.**

Finally, with the amphitheater nearly empty, the two gladiators themselves silently left the arena. History records that, thanks to Telemachus, this was the last gladiator contest held in the entire history of the Roman Empire. One simple man who was committed to "Lordship living" literally changed the fabric of the Roman Empire.[7]

So what's it going to be in your life, my friend? The Christian church is full of "sexy" followers who go for the glamour, the thrills, and the emotion. May you instead spend the rest of your life looking for your "arenas." They'll be there if you just look for them.

Your arena may be at your school, your neighborhood, or with your family and friends. But I guarantee you, **they will always be there.** And your obedience at those secret moments will always create a hell-defying difference. Even more important, you'll be making Jesus lean over heaven and smile.

So in our self-centered Christian world, chart your course with seriousness. In the words of Jesus, don't forget to daily "count the cost." We're not being called to a hard, boring life of rules. But neither did our loving Jesus give His life on the cross to become your "Sexy Savior."

Your rewards? They will echo into all your eternity. Jim Elliot really did have it right:

"He is no fool who gives what he cannot keep... to gain what he cannot lose."

May Jesus Christ not only be your redeeming Savior but forever your beautiful Lord.

"He is no fool who gives what he CANNOT KEEP...to gain what he CANNOT LOSE."

Jim Elliot

Notes:

[1]*Bits & Pieces*, story adapted, *You have to Sin* May, 1991.

[2]*Author would like to recognize that the term "Lord" was also use as a term of respect and not of divinity or discipleship. The original languages and personal intentions of each Lord statement in scripture makes this distinction difficult to give an "exact number." The vastness in contrast of Jesus as Savior in the New Testament to Jesus as Lord (in context) still makes the noted point. If the Old Testament were also used to illustrate this point, the evidence would be overwhelming.*

[3]Rice, Wayne, Opening story adapted, *Alexander the Great – Hot Illustrations for Youth Talks*, Youth Specialties 1993, pg. 18-19, Zondervan, Grand Rapids MI, 49530

[4]Hyde, Douglas, *Dedication and Leadership*, Numerous quoted material, University of Notre Dame Press, Notre Dame, IN 46556, 2007

[5]J.K. Laney, *Marching Orders*, Adapted violin story, pg. 34

[6]Mayo, Jeanne, Adapted *Single Nail* Story, 2009, Multiple other sources

[7]Multiple Sources, Mayo, Jeanne, Christie, Les; Rice Wayne - Adapted story, *Hot Illustrations for Youth Talks*, Youth Specialties 1993, Zondervan, Grand Rapids MI, 49530 pg. 195-196